Walking
Bucks County, Pa.

Country & Town

Walking
Bucks County, Pa.

Country
& Town

Catherine D. Kerr

ISBN 0-9652733-8-5

FREEWHEELING PRESS
P.O. Box 540
Lahaska PA 18931

www.freewheelingpress.com
info@freewheelingpress.com

Special thanks

This book is dedicated to Chris and Sabrina, my loyal walking companions.

With thanks to all who offered advice and shared their favorite walks.

Cover photo by John Hoenstine

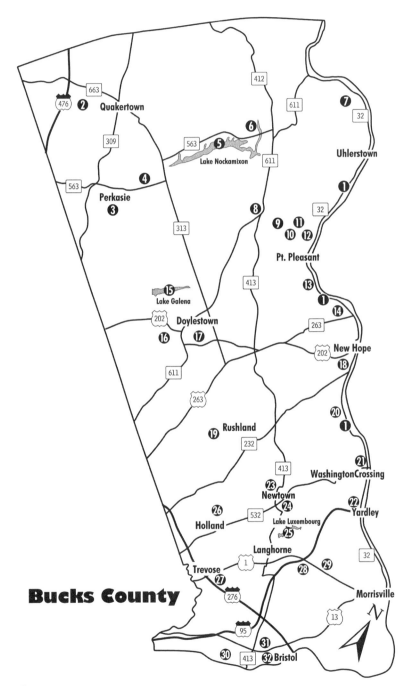

Bucks County

Contents

Introduction

If walking were a recent development, its inventors would be congratulating themselves on devising an activity that serves so many different purposes. Walking is the perfect activity for a multi-tasking world. It's a means of transportation, a method of exercise, a form of recreation. Almost anyone can participate, and it requires little by way of special equipment.

But walking and the appreciation of its many benefits are nothing new. Hippocrates, true to his calling as a physician, called walking "man's best medicine." To Thomas Jefferson, it was "the best possible exercise." The Vietnamese Buddhist monk Thich Nhat Hanh, putting a metaphysical twist on things, wrote that "the true miracle is not walking on water or walking in air, but simply walking on this earth."

Grounded more solidly in the practical, William M. Mitchell, executive director of the Bucks County Department of Parks and Recreation, explained why walking paths are a priority for the department this way: "Walking is probably the number one form of recreation; 87 percent of the American public names walking as their chief form of exercise."

Bucks County, famous for its pastoral scenery, is a wonderful place to walk. From the towpath along the Delaware Canal to quiet country roads to the many well maintained walking paths in its public parks, it offers a variety of settings in which to enjoy every kind of walk, from a vigorous hike to a short stroll.

Walking Bucks County, Pa. tells you all you need to know about a broad selection of Bucks County walks, in a compact but comprehensive form. Some of the walks include a suggested route, but in other cases we have simply tried to give you the information you need to feel confident wandering where you will.

A map and a brief description convey the details of each walk. The maps are designed to help you find the suggested starting point and to keep you from getting lost once you set out. Many of the parks included in this book offer their own detailed trail maps, which complement the information presented here.

The *Walking Bucks County, Pa.* Web site includes hyperlinks to supplementary information for these walks at
www.freewheelingpress.com/walking

A few words of caution

Most of the walks in this book require no special equipment beyond a comfortable pair of shoes. A few follow more rugged trails, where you may prefer to wear hiking books. The descriptive section for each walk will tell you what the terrain is like.

Some of the walks follow country roads, which were included because they carry relatively little motorized traffic. It should be obvious, however, that walking anyplace where cars are also allowed is potentially dangerous. Advisable safety precautions include walking on the left, facing oncoming traffic, so you can see when you need to move aside to let cars go by.

In many parts of Bucks County, ongoing development means that traffic conditions are changing. Take a look around before you start each road walk and decide for yourself if you feel comfortable with the volume of traffic on the road you plan to follow.

Bucks County is part of a broad area where Lyme Disease is a growing health concern. The disease, caused by bacteria, can lead to arthritis and neurological disorders, among other problems. It is transmitted by the tiny deer tick, which is the size of a poppy seed in its nymphal stage and reaches the size of a sesame seed when fully grown.

Because ticks can crawl onto you when you brush against grasses, shrubs, or other vegetation, the American Lyme Disease

Foundation recommends the following precautions to minimize the risk of acquiring the disease:

- Wear enclosed shoes and light-colored clothing with a tight weave to spot ticks easily
- Scan clothes and any exposed skin frequently for ticks while outdoors
- Stay on cleared, well-traveled trails
- Use insect repellant containing DEET (Diethyl-meta-toluamide) on skin or clothes if you intend to go off-trail or into overgrown areas
- Avoid sitting directly on the ground or on stone walls (havens for ticks and their hosts)
- Keep long hair tied back
- Do a final, full-body tick-check at the end of the day (also check children and pets)

Your chances of becoming infected with Lyme Disease are greatly reduced if you remove a tick within the first 24 hours. Early signs of Lyme Disease include flu-like symptoms and a characteristic "bull's-eye" rash, which can occur three days to a month after the tick bite. Consult your health-care professional with any concerns you might have about Lyme Disease.

1. Delaware Canal

No doubt about it, the towpath along the Delaware Canal is one of the nicest places to walk in Bucks County. The path follows the canal for 60 miles, from Bristol to Easton, passing some beautiful scenery along the way. It's surfaced in crushed stone from Uhlerstown to Morrisville, providing an even surface for walking or cycling. Depending on your personal tastes and mood, you can pick a route that will make you feel as if you've left civilization far behind or plan an outing that includes lunch and window-shopping in town.

The canal was constructed in the early 1800s and was in commercial operation for about a century. Supplanted as a means of transportation by the railroads, it became a state park in 1940. The towpath has been designated a National Heritage Hiking Trail.

The canal runs parallel to Route 32 and the Delaware River for most of its length, passing several towns and parks. Though it might seem tempting to start a towpath walk in town, it's often easier to find a place to leave your car in one of the parks. The Virginia Forrest Recreation Area, north of Center Bridge, has handicapped parking as well as restrooms and picnic benches. Tinicum Park on Route 32 near Erwinna and both sections of Washington Crossing State Historic Park (see pages 60 and 64) are also good places to park.

Bridges across the river at Upper Black Eddy, Uhlerstown, Lumberville, Center Bridge, New Hope, and Washington Crossing add the option of parking on the New Jersey side and extending your walk on the path beside New Jersey's Delaware and Raritan

DELAWARE CANAL STATE PARK

Parallels Delaware River, Easton to Bristol

Terrain: Level

Surface: Hard-packed fine stone

Info: 610.982.5560

Canal. The canal paths on both sides of the river are multi-use trails, meaning you might encounter runners, bicyclists, equestrians (in Pennsylvania), and—in the winter months—cross-country skiers.

Because landscapes that include a sweeping view of the water have always had a calming effect on me, I like the towpath best where it runs right next to the river, as it does at Lumberville (see page 42) and just south of Center Bridge. Frenchtown, Lumberville, Stockton, New Hope (see page 56), Lambertville, Yardley (see page 68), and Washington Crossing, N.J., all have places where you can buy refreshments.

New Hope, the busiest of these towns, is popular with tourists who come to browse its many interesting shops and galleries. Just across the river in New Jersey is Lambertville, home to more restaurants and a respectable cluster of antique shops. The Lock Tender's House Visitor Center on the canal at the south end of New Hope has exhibits explaining the history of the canal, and a mule-drawn canal-boat ride is based there during the warmer months. Though the towpath appears to end just south of the visitor center, you can find it again by crossing South Main Street (Route 32), following the gravel road next to the canal all the way through Odette's restaurant parking lot, and crossing the small bridge over the canal just south of Odette's. The towpath narrows to pass a house and some condos before returning to a wooded, undeveloped landscape.

South of Morrisville, the canal turns away from the river and follows busy Route 13 to end in Bristol. This area is highly developed and does not make for pleasant country walking.

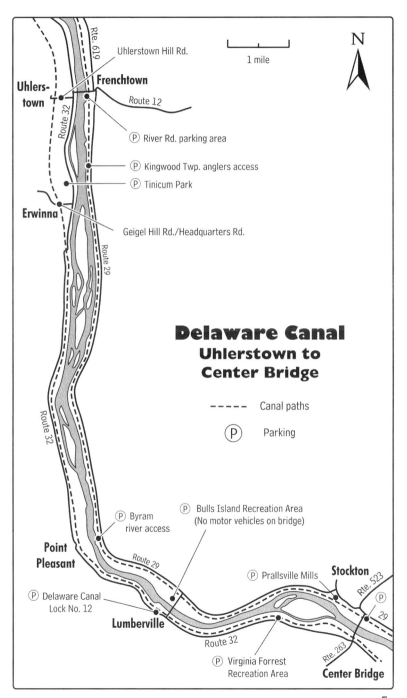

Delaware Canal
Uhlerstown to
Center Bridge

Uhlerstown Hill Rd.

1 mile

N

Rte. 619

Frenchtown

Uhlers-town

Route 32

Route 12

Ⓟ River Rd. parking area

Ⓟ Kingwood Twp. anglers access

Ⓟ Tinicum Park

Erwinna

Geigel Hill Rd./Headquarters Rd.

Route 29

Route 32

- - - - - Canal paths

Ⓟ Parking

Ⓟ Byram river access

Ⓟ Bulls Island Recreation Area (No motor vehicles on bridge)

Point Pleasant

Route 29

Ⓟ Prallsville Mills

Stockton

Rte. 523

Ⓟ Delaware Canal Lock No. 12

Lumberville

Route 32

29

Ⓟ Virginia Forrest Recreation Area

Rte. 263

Center Bridge

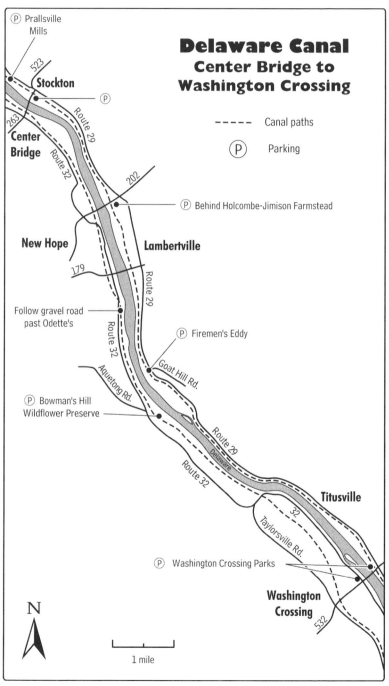

Delaware Canal
Center Bridge to
Washington Crossing

- - - - - Canal paths

(P)   Parking

(P) Prallsville Mills

523

Stockton

(P)

Route 29

263

Center Bridge

Route 32

202

(P) Behind Holcombe-Jimison Farmstead

New Hope

Lambertville

179

Route 29

Follow gravel road past Odette's

Route 32

(P) Firemen's Eddy

Goat Hill Rd.

Aquetong Rd.

(P) Bowman's Hill Wildflower Preserve

Route 29

Delaware

Route 32

Titusville

32

Taylorsville Rd.

(P) Washington Crossing Parks

Washington Crossing

532

N

1 mile

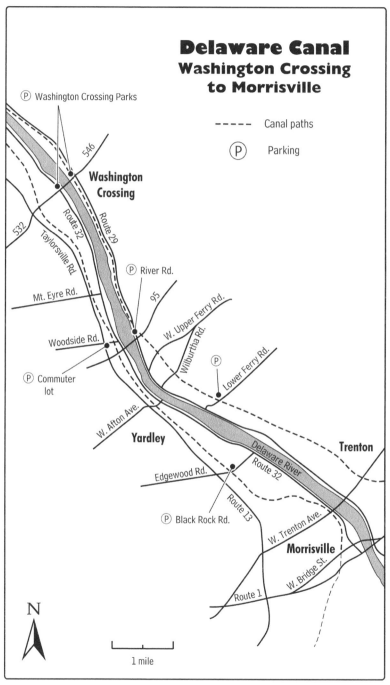

Delaware Canal
Washington Crossing
to Morrisville

- - - - -   Canal paths

Ⓟ   Parking

Ⓟ Washington Crossing Parks

546

**Washington
Crossing**

Route 32

Route 29

532

Taylorsville Rd.

Ⓟ River Rd.

Mt. Eyre Rd.

95

W. Upper Ferry Rd.

Woodside Rd.

Wilburtha Rd.

Ⓟ

Lower Ferry Rd.

Ⓟ Commuter
lot

W. Afton Ave.

Yardley

Delaware River

Trenton

Edgewood Rd.

Route 32

Route 13

Ⓟ Black Rock Rd.

W. Trenton Ave.

Morrisville

W. Bridge St.

Route 1

N

1 mile

2. Mill Road

You won't need sturdy hiking shoes or an extra supply of energy bars to walk Mill Road. It's short and sweet, a side trip into a wooded landscape that is increasingly endangered by encroaching development.

You can leave your car at the Milford Township Park located at the intersection of Mill and Allentown Roads just south of Unami Creek, about three-quarters of a mile south of Milford Square. There isn't much to the park. Its most obvious feature is a flat, rectangular field that is flooded and used as a hockey rink in winter, with some picnic tables nearby.

From there, Mill Road extends about a half mile east to Hillcrest Road. A canopy of trees shades the road as the creek burbles along beside it. The road is quite level, making for a peaceful, pretty walk.

Don't be tempted to create a loop route by following Hillcrest to Foulkes Mill Road, returning via Allentown Road to the park. Allentown is a busy road with no shoulders to walk on, and development near Hillcrest has brought more traffic there, too.

If you're in the mood to go farther, you might do better to cross Allentown and follow Umbreit Road out and back. It's about a mile long, and it's also fairly level as it passes homes built on larger properties in an area dotted with huge boulders.

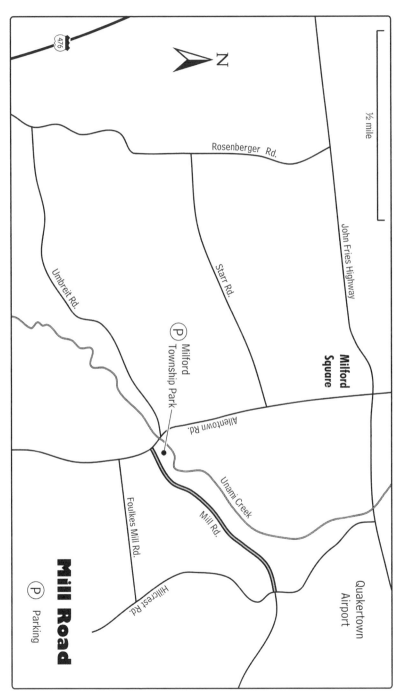

N

476

½ mile

Rosenberger Rd.

John Fries Highway

Starr Rd.

Umbreit Rd.

Milford Square

ⓅMilford Township Park

Allentown Rd.

Unami Creek

Foulkes Mill Rd.

Mill Rd.

Hillcrest Rd.

Mill Road

Ⓟ Parking

Quakertown Airport

3. Perkiomen Creek

Sellersville and Perkasie are next to each other on the map, and it's hard to tell when you've left one and entered the other. The list of things they have in common includes a school district and a pleasantly old-fashioned small-town feeling.

The two towns also share the East Branch of the Perkiomen Creek. They've made the most of some choice real estate along its banks by building several parks that connect seamlessly, with a path for cyclists and pedestrians that is about a mile long and has several loops adding to the total distance you can walk.

Ordinarily, I approach walking on paved paths in town parks with the same sort of enthusiasm I feel for frozen pizza. It isn't necessarily bad, but it's almost never as good as the real thing. Walking here is a pleasure, however. The route past the creek and around various lawns and sports fields is very pretty, and there are benches at frequent points along the path. I passed quite a few others who were out to walk, run, or exercise their dogs and children, yet it never seemed crowded.

The path is detailed in a map that is thoughtfully made available in boxes at either end of the parks. It shows the locations for things like water fountains, picnic tables, and rest rooms, and it lists the mileage for various segments of the route. You don't need a map to keep from getting lost, however, since the path basically runs along the north side of the creek from Main Street in Sellersville to Walnut Street in Perkasie.

LAKE LENAPE PARK, LENAPE PARK

Along East Branch Perkiomen Creek
Sellersville and Perkasie

Terrain: Level

Surface: Paved

Info: 215.257.5075 or 215.257.5065

On the Perkasie end, two small and rather unusual suspension bridges connect the path to an island in the creek and a parking area off Constitution Avenue on the other side. Nearby, there's another interesting bridge that doesn't go anywhere: the Old South Perkasie Covered Bridge, which was built in 1832 and moved to a field at the park in the late 1950s.

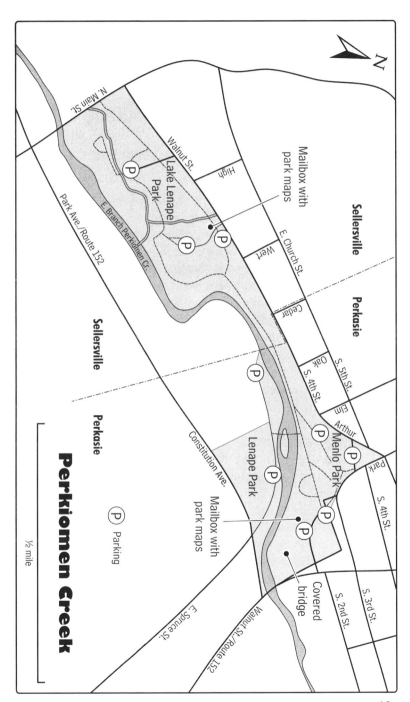

Perkiomen Creek

N

Sellersville

Perkasie

Sellersville

Perkasie

N. Main St.

Walnut St.

Lake Lenape Park

High

E. Branch Perkiomen Cr.

Park Ave./Route 152

E. Church St.

West

Cedar

Oak

S. 5th St.

S. 4th St.

Elm

Arthur

Menlo Park

Park

S. 4th St.

S. 3rd St.

S. 2nd St.

Constitution Ave.

Lenape Park

E. Spruce St.

Walnut St./Route 152

Mailbox with park maps

Mailbox with park maps

Covered bridge

(P) Parking

½ mile

4. East Rockhill Walking Path

The East Rockhill town park, formally known as the Willard H. Markey Centennial Park, includes several sports fields, a driving range that's open in the summer, a children's playground with swings, slides, and climbing equipment, a picnic pavilion, and a paved walking path that stretches 1.2 miles around the perimeter of the complex.

The park is located on Route 563 (Ridge Road) between the East Rockhill municipal building and Pennridge Airport, a little over a mile from the intersection of Routes 563 and 313.

The walking path, which is wide and level, begins at the end of the parking lot next to the children's play area. Once you're on the path, you really can't lose your way. An auto junkyard is visible through the trees close to the start, and I must admit that it had the effect of diminishing some of my enthusiasm for the walk as I was setting out. Once you make the first turn, however, the view consists of corn-fields and a distant tree-covered ridge in addition to the park facilities.

If you're looking to walk or run a measured route of about a mile away from traffic, this is the place for you. This very businesslike path does lack a little something in atmosphere, however, even after you pass the junkyard. Also, it offers very little shade, so if you plan to walk here on a hot day, you'll probably want to do so early in the morning or toward evening when the sun starts to go down.

EAST ROCKHILL TOWNSHIP WALKING PATH

Ridge Rd. (Rte. 563) between the East Rockhill municipal building and Pennridge Airport
near Perkasie

Terrain: Level

Surface: Paved

Info: 215.257.9156

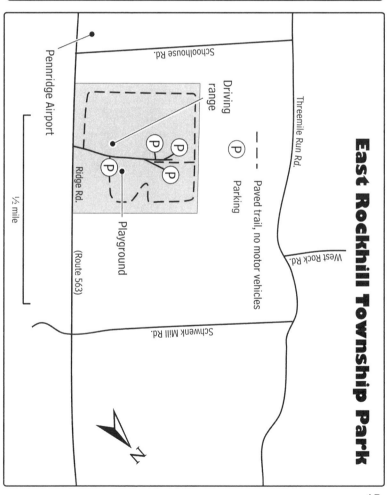

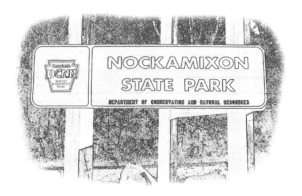

5. Lake Nockamixon

Lake Nockamixon is probably better known for boating and fishing than as a place to go walking, but scenery this lovely surely belongs on any list of good places to walk in Bucks County.

Located about four miles east of Quakertown, the lake is seven miles long and is surrounded by state parkland. Because Nockamixon State Park is so large, it has several entrances. The main day use area, located south of the park office off Route 563 (Mountain View Drive), is open from April to October. Other areas are open all year.

There are four boat-launch areas on the lake, including a marina with docking space for 576 boats, as well as a boat rental concession offering canoes, motorboats, rowboats, sailboats, paddleboats, and pontoon boats. The park also has a swimming pool (swimming in the lake is forbidden), equestrian trails, hundreds of picnic tables, and family cabins that are available for rent.

As far as I'm concerned, however, nothing beats the simple enjoyment of the view of the blue lake and the distant hills around it, which is as pretty on a clear winter day as it is in summer when colorful sails bob along the water. I like to walk along the paved bicycle path, which runs about a mile along the shoreline from the jetty near the marina to the park's fishing pier. Those interested in more traditional hiking can find it here, too, on the trails located between Route 563 and the lake near the Weisel Youth Hostel, toward the southwestern end of the park.

NOCKAMIXON STATE PARK

Between Mountain View Dr. (Rte. 563) and Ridge Rd. near Quakertown

Schedule: Day use area (south of the park office) open from April 1 through Octotber 31; other areas open all year

Terrain: Level to moderately hilly

Surface: Paved path, woodland trails

At the other end, the park abuts State Game Lands No. 157, which includes Haycock Mountain (see page 20).

You can pick up a detailed map of the park facilities at the park headquarters on Route 563. Park officials have been planning major renovations to the swimming pool, so you should call to confirm that it's open if you plan to swim.

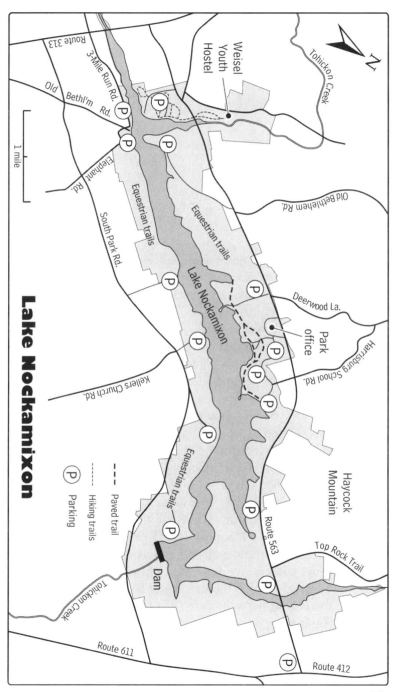

Lake Nockamixon

Weisel Youth Hostel

Tohickon Creek

Route 313

3-Mile Run Rd.

Old Bethl'm Rd.

1 mile

Elephant Rd.

Old Bethlehem Rd.

South Park Rd.

Equestrian trails

Equestrian trails

Lake Nockamixon

Deerwood La.

Park office

Harrisburg School Rd.

Kellers Church Rd.

Haycock Mountain

Equestrian trails

Route 563

Top Rock Trail

Dam

Tohickon Creek

Route 611

Route 412

- - - Paved trail

----- Hiking trails

P Parking

19

6. Haycock Run Road

Just north of Lake Nockamixon, a little stream called Haycock Creek meanders along the base of Haycock Mountain on its way to the lake. This is a wooded area with small houses widely spaced along a quiet country road.

State Game Lands No. 157 includes cone-shaped Haycock Mountain and has a parking lot that makes a convenient starting point for two walks, an easy road walk following the creek and a shorter but more challenging trail up the side of the mountain to an overlook with a view of the lake when the leaves are off the trees.

The game lands parking area is north of Route 563 on Top Rock Trail, which is marked by a large sign for St. John the Baptist Church. (The historically minded may be interested to know that it is the oldest Catholic parish in Bucks County.) When Top Rock Trail bends to the right, you'll find the game lands parking on the left.

It's just over 2.75 relatively level miles from the game lands parking lot to the end of Haycock Run Road at Stony Garden Road.

The trail up Haycock Mountain leads from the game lands parking lot past the taller of the mountain's two peaks, which tops out at about 960 feet and has the distinction of being the highest mountain located wholly within Bucks County. (Another mountain that straddles the border between Bucks and Northampton Counties is about 20 feet higher.) As the name implies, the game lands are publicly owned areas set aside primarily for hunting, although other activities including hiking are allowed.

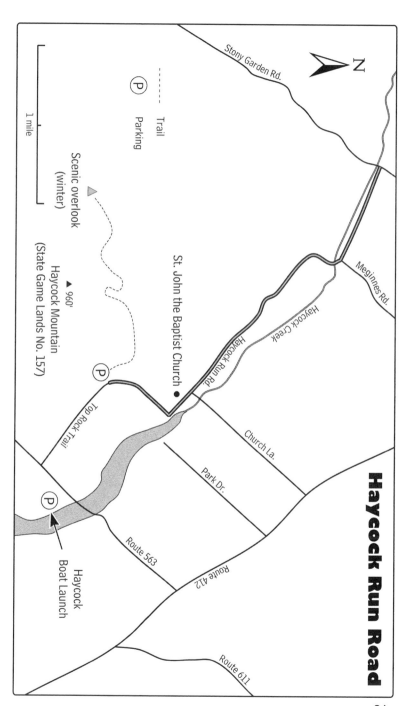

Haycock Run Road

N

Stony Garden Rd.

Meginnes Rd.

Haycock Creek

Haycock Run Rd.

Church La.

Park Dr.

Route 563

Route 412

Route 611

St. John the Baptist Church

Top Rock Trail

▲ 960'
Haycock Mountain
(State Game Lands No. 157)

Scenic overlook
(winter)

---- Trail

(P) Parking

1 mile

(P)

(P)

Haycock
Boat Launch

7. Ringing Rocks

Ringing Rocks Park has to be one of the strangest parks in Bucks County.

The main attraction is an eight-acre field of huge reddish boulders, a peculiar enough sight in itself. Odder still is the fact that many of the rocks ring like bells when struck. On a busy day at the park, you'll find most of your fellow hikers trudging toward the boulder field with hammers in hand, looking like a troop of single-minded carpenters on their way to a remote job site. No matter where you go the woods resound with the chinking metallic sound of the rocks being struck, often accompanied by peals of delighted laughter.

If you want to make some rock music yourself, bring your own hammer. Some of the boulders produce better sounds than others; these are easy to find because they have large worn patches created by repeated banging over the years.

Ringing Rocks Park is a little off the beaten path in the northeastern corner of Bucks County. To get there from Route 32, take Uhlerstown Hill Road, which is just north of the bridge from Upper Black Eddy to Milford, N.J Go about a mile and a half to Ringing Rocks Road, which is marked with a sign for the park. Turn right onto Ringing Rocks Road, and you'll find the park on your right.

On a many a quieter day, you'll find that you have the place more or less to yourself, and you can decide whether to linger at the boulder field or continue down the trail to the waterfall, which is touted by tourism literature as Bucks County's largest.

RINGING ROCKS PARK

Ringing Rocks Road
near Upper Black Eddy

Terrain: Gently sloping to boulder fields; some steep sections near waterfall

Surface: Woodland trails

Info: 215.757.0571

A single trail leaves the parking lot at the opposite end from the entrance driveway. It soon splits into two. The left fork leads to the bottom of the boulder field, and the right fork continues past the boulder field into the woods. You'll find the waterfall roughly a third of a mile from the parking area. From here it's possible to turn to the right and cross the stream above the falls, follow the stream back down past the falls, recross the creek, and return to the main trail, but the climb back is somewhat steep.

There is no real trail across the boulder field, but it is possible to climb from boulder to boulder. This is a great place to bring agile children to work off some energy, but you'll want to keep the clumsier ones close to level ground, since there is some potential for getting hurt by falling on the rocks.

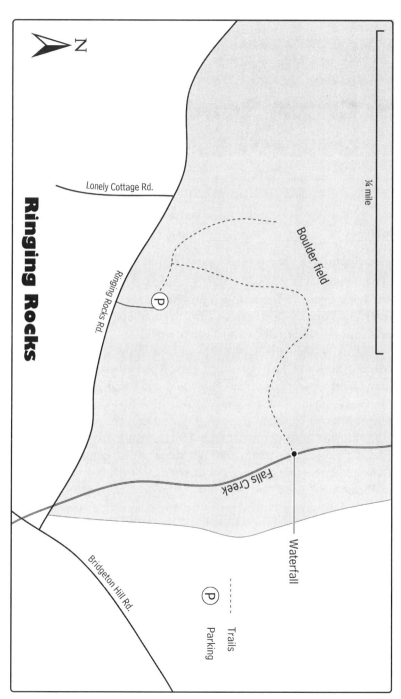

Ringing Rocks

Lonely Cottage Rd.

Ringing Rocks Rd.

Boulder field

¼ mile

Falls Creek

Bridgeton Hill Rd.

Waterfall

- - - - - Trails

Ⓟ Parking

N

25

8. Creek Road

Creek Road is one of those Bucks County treasures that seems to be hidden away in plain sight. It intersects busy Route 611 about nine miles north of Doylestown, yet I drove past it in ignorance for years. Then one day, for reasons I can't remember, I decided to turn onto it and found myself in a different world.

As luck would have it, there's a small cleared area on the west side of Route 611 just north of Creek Road where you can leave your car. Walk west on Creek Road and you'll find yourself following Deep Run, a relatively small stream that flows under 611 and joins the larger Tohickon Creek on the other side.

Although the land rises steeply to your right, the road itself is level. It follows the stream through some pretty countryside past farms and into the woods, and it doesn't carry much traffic.

About a mile and a third from Route 611, the road crosses a branch of the creek, bends to the left, and comes to a stop sign. Go through this intersection, which is Rolling Hills Road, and turn right onto Creek Road to continue along Deep Run. The landscape remains much the same here, although the cliff to the north is even steeper. A little over a mile and a half from Route 611, you'll reach another stop sign at Quarry Road (not surprisingly the site of an old quarry). After this, Creek Road starts to go uphill as it heads into Bedminster.

Walk as far as you like, then turn around and retrace your steps to where you began.

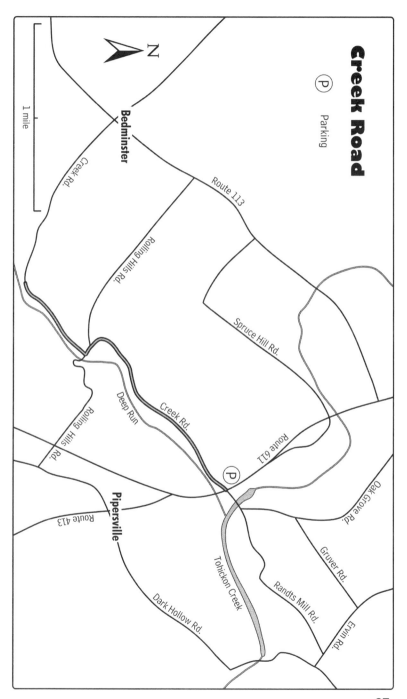

Creek Road

Ⓟ Parking

N

1 mile

Bedminster

Creek Rd.

Route 113

Rolling Hills Rd.

Spruce Hill Rd.

Deep Run

Creek Rd.

Route 611

Rolling Hills Rd.

Pipersville

Route 413

Oak Grove Rd.

Ⓟ

Tohickon Creek

Gruver Rd.

Randts Mill Rd.

Dark Hollow Rd.

Elvin Rd.

9. Covered Bridge Road

Covered Bridge Road makes a pleasant stroll between the Cabin Run Covered Bridge and the Stover-Myers Mill.

The easiest way to find it is to turn onto Dark Hollow Road from Route 413 at the last intersection before 413 ends at Route 611. Follow Dark Hollow about 1.1 miles to Covered Bridge Road. The mill is operated as a county park, and it has a generous parking area across the street from a field where sheep graze in front of a classic red barn.

The mill building is in the process of being restored, and it is open only during limited hours in the summer. It's still worth a look around, however. It was built around 1800 by Jacob Stover and was originally powered by water from Tohickon Creek, which flows behind it. It continued to be used well into the twentieth century and is listed on the National Register of Historic Places.

Covered Bridge Road starts by the mill and runs right beside the creek. The road itself is fairly level, although the land rises steeply on either side. It's a little over half a mile from the mill to the covered bridge, which spans Cabin Run, a tributary of Tohickon Creek. The bridge is a classic built in 1871, a typical red-and-white wooden bridge of the sort still being used at a number of places around Bucks County. You can continue walking on the other side of the bridge, although the road turns steeply uphill from here. Go as far as you like, then turn around and retrace the route back to the mill.

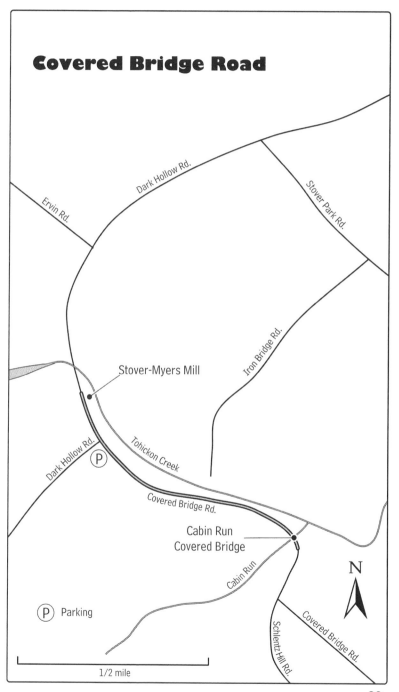

Covered Bridge Road

Dark Hollow Rd.

Ervin Rd.

Stover Park Rd.

Iron Bridge Rd.

Stover-Myers Mill

Dark Hollow Rd.

Tohickon Creek

(P)

Covered Bridge Rd.

Cabin Run
Covered Bridge

Cabin Run

N

(P) Parking

Schlentz Hill Rd.

Covered Bridge Rd.

1/2 mile

10. Ralph Stover State Park

Not far from Point Pleasant, Tohickon Creek bends back on itself in a couple of sharp horseshoe curves and flows past some strikingly tall cliffs before it straightens out again and joins the Delaware River.

Ralph Stover State Park is one of a series of state and county parks grouped along the creek in this area, which is a well known destination for rock climbers, hikers, whitewater kayakers, and sightseers who come to admire the view.

Stover Park is located at creek level in a cool, shaded area where children are tempted to stick their toes in the water while their parents talk or walk nearby. There are cabins for family camping as well as picnic facilities and some short trails along the creek, all shown on the official park map. An attractive pedestrian bridge crosses the Tohickon here, leading to Stover Park Road, which goes up toward the other parks. The park also has a boat-launch area used by whitewater enthusiasts during the twice-yearly whitewater releases from Lake Nockamixon upstream, although the rest of the time, the rocky creek is much more tame.

If you're interested in a short, fairly level walk, stay on the trails near the picnic areas. For a longer, more serious walk, cross the bridge and head up Stover Park Road. The road is steep, but because it is essentially a dead end, there isn't much traffic here. Near Tory Road, you can pick up the trail to the High Rocks Vista and Tohickon Valley Park. (See pages 34 and 38.)

RALPH STOVER STATE PARK

State Park Rd.
near Point Pleasant

Terrain: Level along creek; steep elsewhere

Surface: Woodland trails, roads

Info: 610.982.5560

To find Ralph Stover State Park, turn onto Tohickon Hill Road at the intersection of Route 32 and Point Pleasant Pike in Point Pleasant. Bear right onto State Park Road after about three-quarters of a mile and follow it to the park, which is located about two miles from Point Pleasant.

Iron Bridge Road

If you prefer a road walk, stay on Stover Park Road until you reach Iron Bridge Road, which goes off to the left. Although some maps still show a bridge at the foot of Iron Bridge Road crossing Tohickon Creek and connecting to Covered Bridge Road, the bridge is long gone, so Iron Bridge Road is also a dead end.

It's about a mile from the bridge at Ralph Stover State Park to Iron Bridge Road, and not quite that far from there to the end of Iron Bridge. The first half-mile or so of Iron Bridge is relatively level as it passes through some pretty open farmland, although after that it does become somewhat steep.

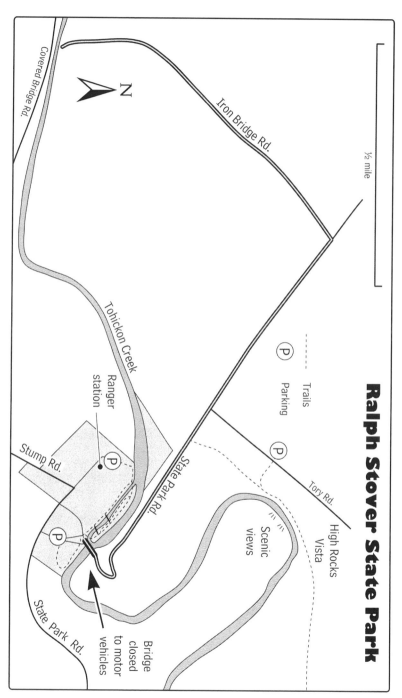

Ralph Stover State Park

N

½ mile

Covered Bridge Rd.

Iron Bridge Rd.

Tohickon Creek

Ranger station

Stump Rd.

State Park Rd.

State Park Rd.

Tory Rd.

High Rocks Vista

Scenic views

Bridge closed to motor vehicles

------ Trails

Ⓟ Parking

11. High Rocks

The view from High Rocks Vista is one of the best and most unusual in Bucks County. From atop a cliff that rises some 200 feet above Tohickon Creek, you can look down to the creek or out at a sweeping view of the surrounding woods.

The last time I visited the vista, it was a bright fall day when the variations in color seemed to highlight the individual leaves on the trees in the valley far below. Two young people stood kissing on one of the footpaths as if they were alone, which was almost the case, since I didn't hang around. When I reached the first lookout, a turkey vulture came soaring toward me at about eye level, and just when I was sure I'd have to duck to keep it from flying straight into my face, it turned away to follow the course of the creek. I looked down and saw other birds flying over the water in a top-down view that reminded me of flying over an airport where planes were taking off and landing far below.

The rocky face of the cliff is popular with climbers who know what they're doing (there's a fence at the edge of the lookout meant to protect those like me who don't). The trail above the cliff is part of one of the most popular hiking routes in the county (see page 38). Trails in the state park areas are shown on the Ralph Stover State Park map.

To reach High Rocks, turn onto Cafferty Road from Route 32 in Point Pleasant and go about a mile and three-quarters to Tory Road. Turn left onto Tory and stay left when Wormansville Road goes off

HIGH ROCKS VISTA

Tory Rd.
near Point Pleasant

Terrain: Slightly downhill on trail to vista; level to gently rolling on roads

Surface: Woodland trails, roads

Info: 610.982.5560

to the right. The High Rocks parking area will be on your right about a mile and a quarter from Cafferty Road.

Tory Road

You can make a fairly pleasant road walk by turning left onto Tory Road from the High Rocks parking area. The full loop shown on the map follows Tory to Municipal, Smithtown, and Wormansville Roads, passing through the village of Tinicum at the intersection of Smithtown and Wormansville. It totals about three and a half miles, although a shorter out-and-back walk on Tory is also possible.

Tory Road is wooded and unpaved until just before it reaches Wormansville. The rest of the route is paved and passes woods, houses, and some farmland. The terrain on these roads ranges from level to rolling to slightly uphill. There's usually little traffic on this route, although you'll see more once you leave Tory Road.

(See page 30 for information on walking from nearby Ralph Stover State Park.)

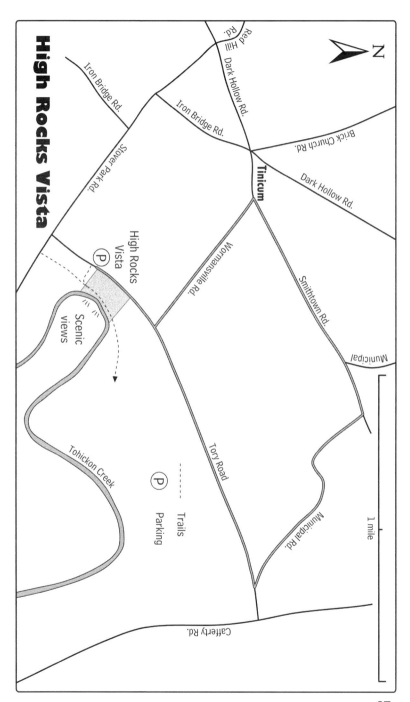

High Rocks Vista

N

Red Hill Rd.

Iron Bridge Rd.

Dark Hollow Rd.

Iron Bridge Rd.

Brick Church Rd.

Stover Park Rd.

Tinicum

Dark Hollow Rd.

High Rocks Vista

Ⓟ

Wormansville Rd.

Scenic views

Smithtown Rd.

Municipal

Tohickon Creek

Tory Road

------ Trails

Ⓟ Parking

Municipal Rd.

1 mile

Cafferty Rd.

37

12. Tohickon Valley

Though the walk described in this chapter goes through state and county parkland along Tohickon Creek, it's definitely not what you'd call a stroll in the park. The trails follow the contours of the steep creek banks and come closer to serious hiking than many of the other routes described in this book.

It's only about a mile and a half from Tohickon Valley Park to the High Rocks Vista and its striking views, but those who feel they're just getting started at this distance can go farther by adding several other walks in the area (see pages 30 and 34).

You can start this walk at Tohickon Valley Park, a Bucks County facility, or at High Rocks Vista, which is operated by the state of Pennsylvania. The main trail connecting the two sites is known as the red trail, and it's marked by a white square with a red center. Another trail, blazed in white, runs parallel over part of the distance, so it's possible to go out on one of the trails and return on the other, though the views and terrain are quite similar.

To get to Tohickon Valley Park, turn off Route 32 onto Cafferty Road in Point Pleasant. It's about a mile from there to the park, which will be on your left. If the group camping area in the Deer Wood Campground section of Tohickon Valley Park is not in use, you can park there. Otherwise, you'll have to leave your car near the swimming pool in the main area of the park and walk to the campground (see map; the pool is open May 30 to Labor Day, with a higher entrance fee for non-Bucks residents).

TOHICKON VALLEY PARK

Cafferty Road
near Point Pleasant

Terrain: Hilly

Surface: Woodland trails

Info: .215.757.0571

To locate the start of the red trail, look for a group of picnic tables in the middle of a small clearing by the group camping area. The trail begins at a chain gate located past the tables at the edge of the clearing. Beyond the camping area, you'll come to a place where you have to turn right to stay on the red trail; it's clearly marked.

The white trail begins at the end of the unpaved road through the camping area. Walk to the end of the road and keep going, and you'll be on the trail. Both the red and white trails cross several small streams before reaching a spot where you can switch from one to the other. The connecting trail passes between a pair of trees marked with white circles.

To start at High Rocks, follow the directions above, turning onto Cafferty Road from Route 32 in Point Pleasant. Go past Tohickon Valley Park to Tory Road, about a mile and three-quarters from Route 32. Turn left onto Tory and stay left when Wormansville Road goes off to the right. The High Rocks parking area will be on your right about a mile and a quarter from Cafferty Road.

Cross Tory Road from the parking area and follow the trail down to the Argillite Overlook at the edge of the cliff above the Tohickon. This area is popular with rock climbers, so don't be surprised if you find people working their way up the steep cliff. (And don't drop anything near the edge.) The trail toward Tohickon Valley Park runs parallel to the edge of the cliff here, and it is blazed with white, although the familiar red-in-white marks soon appear. You'll find several other protected overlooks farther along the trail as you walk toward Tohickon Valley.

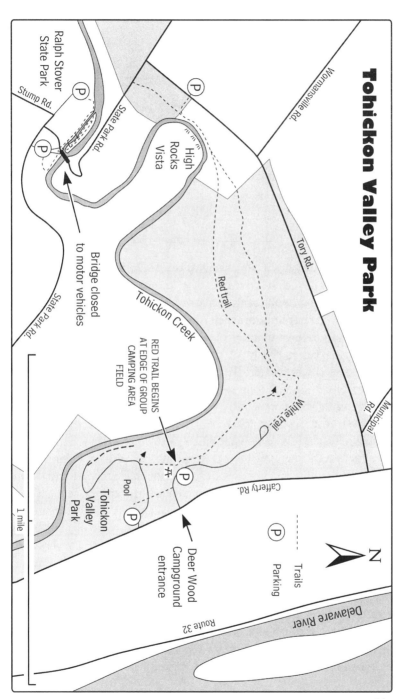

Tohickon Valley Park

Ralph Stover
State Park

Stump Rd.

State Park Rd.

High
Rocks
Vista

Bridge closed
to motor vehicles

Tohickon Creek

State Park Rd.

RED TRAIL BEGINS
AT EDGE OF GROUP
CAMPING AREA
FIELD

Red trail

White trail

Tohickon
Valley
Park

Pool

Deer Wood
Campground
entrance

Cafferty Rd.

Wormansville Rd.

Tory Rd.

Municipal Rd.

Route 32

Delaware River

1 mile

N

------ Trails

Ⓟ Parking

41

13. Fleecydale Road

The Paunacussing Creek descends to the Delaware River through a narrow valley that connects the towns of Carversville and Lumberville. Two small roads also follow that route: Fleecydale Road, which hugs the edge of the creek rather closely, and Old Carversville Road, which follows the contours of the valley just above it.

Neither road carries much traffic. While Fleecydale goes steadily uphill toward Carversville, it is a gentle climb and a favorite with walkers and cyclists. A long section of Old Carversville Road is unpaved and drivers find it narrow and somewhat rough, though this shouldn't be a problem for walkers. Old Carversville does have a couple hills, and it is somewhat steeply downhill when it comes into Lumberville through the lumberyard that gave the town its name.

Because of this, it's probably best to walk up Fleecydale and down Old Carversville if you are planning to make the complete loop. The route from town to town and back again totals about five miles, although you can cut about a mile off that by turning directly from Fleecydale onto Old Carversville, bypassing the town of Carversville. (Of course, you can make your walk shorter still by going out as far as you wish on Fleecydale and returning the same way.)

Each of these towns basically is a general store and a cluster of houses. There are a few parking spaces next to the canal in Lumberville, although the best place to park is at the Bull's Island Recreation Area in New Jersey, which is connected to Lumberville via a pedestrian bridge across the Delaware.

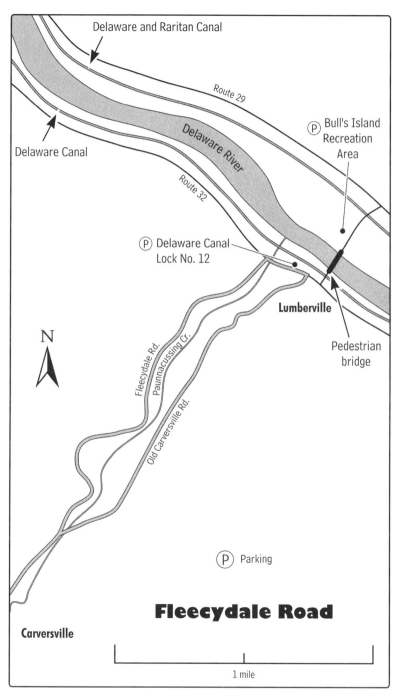

Delaware and Raritan Canal

Route 29

Delaware River

Delaware Canal

Route 32

Ⓟ Bull's Island Recreation Area

Ⓟ Delaware Canal Lock No. 12

Lumberville

Pedestrian bridge

N

Fleecydale Rd.

Paunnacussing Cr.

Old Carversville Rd.

Ⓟ Parking

Fleecydale Road

Carversville

1 mile

14. Laurel Road

Just north of Center Bridge, Route 32 passes between a flat sweep of river lowland and a steep bank covered with rhododendrons. Laurel Road is easy to miss and that might be a good thing, because the feeling of being off the beaten path is definitely part of its charm.

It's an unpaved road that climbs from the river under a magnificent arch of trees. There's a small stream to the north and woods to the south, marked as a nature preserve protected by the Heritage Conservancy. Shafts of sunlight slice through the trees, and you'll almost certainly hear birdsong as you walk.

The nicest part of Laurel is the mile or so between River Road (Route 32) and Comfort Road, but if you're in the mood you can keep walking from there. These roads are paved and there's a little more traffic, but it's still lovely countryside. I like to turn right on Comfort and go as far as my mood takes me. If you're feeling energetic, follow Comfort to Paxson and turn right, descending along another stream to the river. Unfortunately, the stretch of River Road between Paxson and Laurel carries high-speed traffic and there's no shoulder, so you'll have to return to Laurel the way you came. If you're feeling even more energetic, go all the way over to Cuttalossa Road, another scenic country road that is one of my favorites.

Laurel is not quite half a mile north of the intersection of Routes 32 and 263 in Center Bridge. There's a small cleared area on Route 32 at the foot of Laurel where you can leave your car, as long as you make sure it's completely out of the way of traffic.

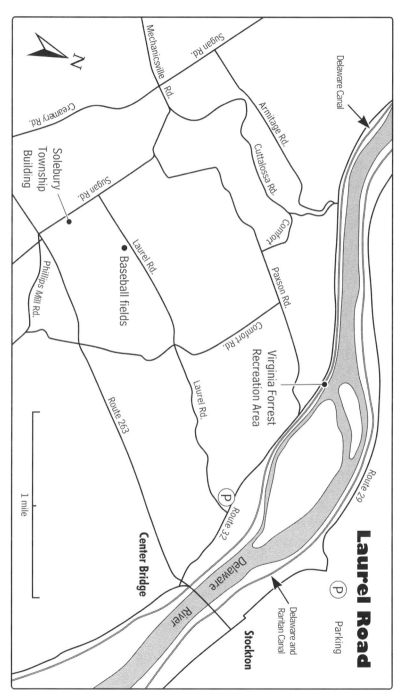

Laurel Road

Ⓟ Parking

45

15. Peace Valley Park

For walkers, Peace Valley Park is the crown jewel in the Bucks County park system.

The park surrounds Lake Galena, a narrow lake more than two miles long that is bounded by hills rising to the north and south. Its facilities include picnic areas for groups large and small, a boat-launch ramp, boat rentals, fishing piers, and children's play areas. For walkers, however, Peace Valley's trails (and their glorious views) are the park's defining feature.

Peace Valley has fourteen miles of unpaved nature trails as well as a paved bike/hike path that goes most of the way around the lake. The paved path is generally level, as are many of the nature trails, although a few of these do get a little hilly. A map showing details of the nature trails, located mostly at the eastern end of the lake, is available at the nature center. Suggested loops range from ten to sixty minutes in walking time and extend through woods, meadows, and wetlands. Some of the trails closest to the nature center building are surfaced in gravel, and all of the trails are marked and groomed.

For years, the park's main shortcoming was the fact that the bike/hike trail did not go all the way around the lake. In two places, trail users got dumped from the paved trail out onto the road. The short stretch of Creek Road on the south side of the lake was never a big problem because it doesn't carry much traffic anyway. But that was hardly the case between the main park entrance on New Galena Road and the nature center on Chapman Road. Anyone who wanted

PEACE VALLEY PARK

Creek Rd.
New Britain Township

Schedule: Nature center building open 9 A.M. to 5 P.M. Tuesday through Sunday

Terrain: Paved paths mostly level; some hills on trails

Surface: Paved and gravel paths, woodland trails

Info: .215.822.8608

to bike, run, or walk the full six-mile circuit on pavement eventually ended up traveling those roads.

Although New Galena isn't exactly a major highway, it doesn't have any shoulder and it does carry a fair amount of traffic. On fair-weather weekends, with cars weaving in and out to avoid heavy pedestrian and bicycle traffic, it began to resemble the sidewalk in a crazy place without roads. To remedy the situation, the county planned to finish an extension of the paved path in that area by the spring of 2002.

In the meantime, it's still possible to avoid that section of road by walking on two nature trails. Assuming you are traveling in a clockwise direction, follow the bike/hike trail around to the parking lot near the north park entrance at New Galena Road. Pick up the West Woods Trail, which goes off to the right (toward the lake) from the driveway between the parking lot and New Galena Road. When the West Woods Trail ends, follow the Sunrise Trail back to the nature center area. Cross the lake and return to the bike/hike path.

The Peace Valley Nature Center and the main park entrance can both be reached by turning onto New Galena Road from Route 313 and following signs, but there are other parking lots at various points around the lake.

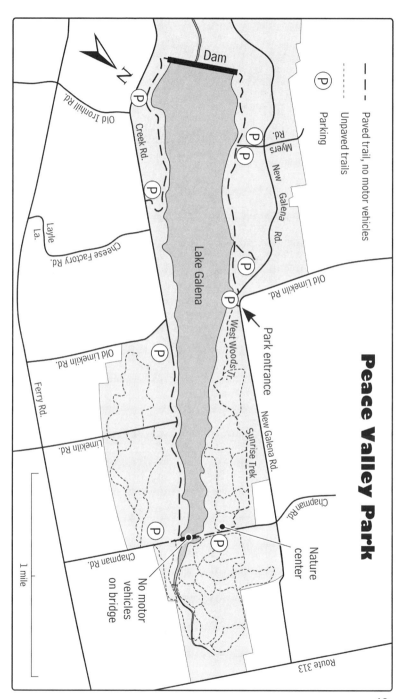

Peace Valley Park

Legend:
- – – Paved trail, no motor vehicles
- .... Unpaved trails
- Ⓟ Parking

Lake Galena

Dam

N

Old Ironhill Rd.
Creek Rd.
Myers Rd.
New Galena Rd.
Layle La.
Cheese Factory Rd.
Old Limekiln Rd.
Park entrance
West Woods Tr.
Old Limekiln Rd.
Ferry Rd.
Limekiln Rd.
Sunrise Trek
New Galena Rd.
Chapman Rd.
Nature center
Chapman Rd.
No motor vehicles on bridge
Route 313

1 mile

16. Central Park

When I first heard that Doylestown Township had a recreation facility called Central Park, I thought it sounded a little pretentious, like an aspiring teenage band calling itself the Rolling Stones. New York City's Central Park is so big and so well known that any other place by that name would have to seem dinky in comparison.

Doylestown's Central Park is surrounded by housing developments instead of skyscrapers, it has no Sheep Meadow and no zoo, and it shares a site with the Doylestown Township Building rather than the Metropolitan Museum of Art, but it's a big place by local standards. The 108-acre park has lighted tennis and basketball courts, a picnic pavilion, soccer fields, a golf tee, an amphitheater, a mile and a half of paved paths, and a collection of marked, unpaved trails through the woods at the top of a hill. It's a busy place where township officials are doing their best to keep up with the recreational needs of a growing population.

The park's best-known feature, at least in certain circles, is its Kids' Castle, a rambling eight-story wooden play structure opened in 1997 after a massive community organizing effort. (The castle is closed in winter and doesn't reopen until April 15, and the township is adamant about enforcing this regulation.)

On sunny mornings in any season, exercise walkers flock to its paved paths, which are level along Wells Road and around the sports fields but climb uphill along the edge of the woods past Kids' Castle. A twenty-one-station exercise circuit lines the path.

CENTRAL PARK

Wells Rd.
Doylestown

Terrain: Level near road, sports fields, and Kids' Castle;
hilly near woods

Surface: Paved paths, woodland trails

Info: 215.348.9915

The unpaved trails are groomed and marked with color-coded signs that match a map posted on a board at the trail entrance nearest the parking area. Split-log benches have been placed at intervals along the trails. The maps are a convenience, and these trails make for pleasant walking, but there really isn't any serious danger that you'll get lost here.

The park is located on Wells Road off Lower State Road, not far from Delaware Valley College and just south of the big cloverleaf intersection of Routes 611 and 202.

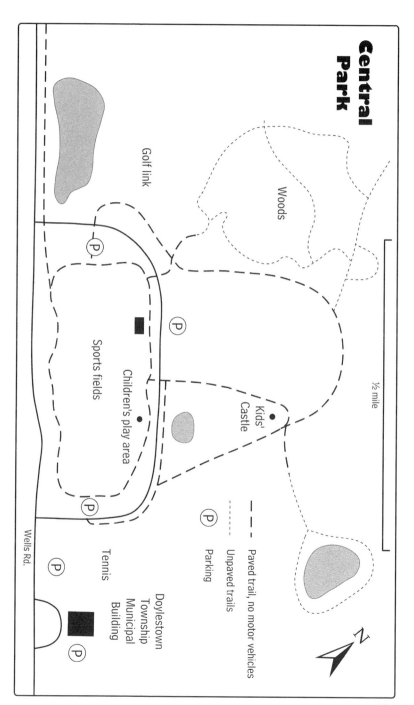

Central Park

Golf link

Woods

Sports fields

Children's play area

Kids' Castle

½ mile

Wells Rd.

Tennis

Doylestown Township Municipal Building

(P) Parking

– – – Paved trail, no motor vehicles

········ Unpaved trails

N

53

17. Doylestown

Doylestown is a great walking town, the kind of place where you can park your car once and go from a museum to a restaurant to a movie and out for coffee afterwards without having to drive anywhere until you're ready to go home.

It's also perfect for a leisurely Sunday afternoon walk of the sort I envision taking with one very good friend. This suggested route for such an outing takes you past the county courthouse to the sites known locally as "the Mercer Mile."

Henry Chapman Mercer, the eccentric collector who died in 1930, evidently was fascinated with reinforced concrete, and he built three structures using it. The forty-five-room Fonthill (215.348.9461), which Mercer used as his residence (with 10 bathrooms!) and also as a showplace for his vast collection of tiles from around the world, is at one end of Doylestown, next to the Moravian Pottery & Tileworks (215.345.6722), where he produced his own distinctive tiles.

Across town you'll find the Mercer Museum (215.345.0210), which houses his collection of pre-industrial tools. Nearby is the James A. Michener Art Museum (215.340.9800), located in the former county jail, which has an excellent collection of regional artists.

If you want to know more about what you're seeing as you stroll, you can pick up a walking tour from the Central Bucks Chamber of Commerce (115 W. Court St., 215.348.3913). The brochure includes detailed information about the sites on three different walks in Doylestown.

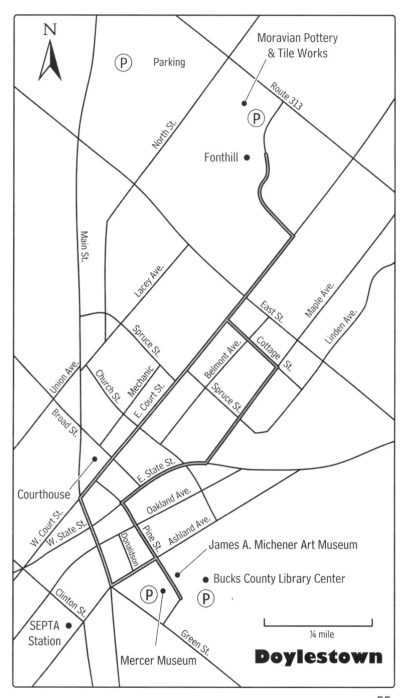

N

P Parking

Moravian Pottery & Tile Works

Route 313

P

Fonthill

North St.

Main St.

Lacey Ave.

East St.

Maple Ave.

Linden Ave.

Spruce St.

Belmont Ave.

Cottage St.

Church St.

Mechanic

E. Court St.

Spruce St.

Union Ave.

Broad St.

E. State St.

Courthouse

Oakland Ave.

W. Court St.

W. State St.

Donaldson

Pine St.

Ashland Ave.

James A. Michener Art Museum

Bucks County Library Center

P

Clinton St.

P

SEPTA Station

Green St.

Mercer Museum

¼ mile

Doylestown

18. New Hope

New Hope is popular with day-trippers who come to shop, eat, and stroll. It's a compact town centered on a half-mile stretch of Main Street. Once known as an artists' colony, it still has plenty of art both public and private, from gallery collections to large public artworks including William Selesnick's canal murals near the mule-barge ride at the south end of Main Street and Robert Rosenwald's sculpture *Sign of the Times* next to the bridge to Lambertville, N.J.

I haven't recommended any particular route because I think it's better to explore as your own personal interests drive you. If you need further guidance, visit the information center at South Main and Mechanic Streets (215.862.5880). And if New Hope isn't enough, consider crossing the Delaware River to Lambertville, which has more restaurants and shops, including several used bookstores and quite a few antiques shops.

Parking is mostly metered and in short supply at peak periods in both towns. The sidewalks can be crowded on weekend afternoons, too, so consider visiting on weekdays or weekend mornings if you're serious about walking.

For a country walk, go west on Mechanic Street past Stockton Avenue, which follows Ingham Creek and the New Hope & Ivyland Railroad tracks through a wooded landscape made famous by the primitive artist Joseph Pickett in his painting called *Manchester Valley*. There is some traffic but not much after you leave town. Go as far as you like, then turn around and retrace your route.

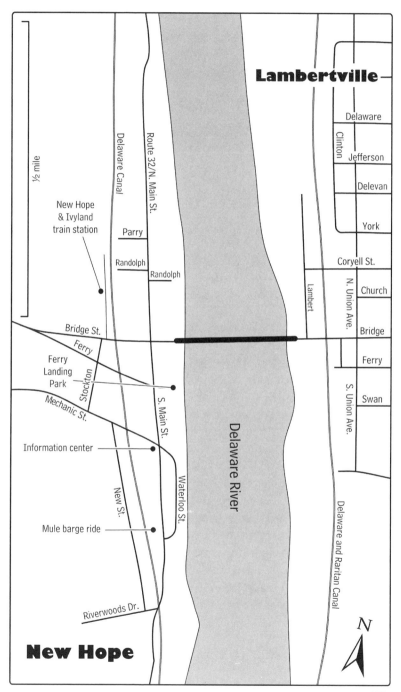

Lambertville

Delaware

Clinton

Jefferson

Delevan

York

Coryell St.

Church

Bridge

Ferry

Swan

N. Union Ave.

S. Union Ave.

Lambert

Delaware and Raritan Canal

Delaware River

½ mile

New Hope & Ivyland train station

Delaware Canal

Route 32/N. Main St.

Parry

Randolph

Randolph

Bridge St.

Ferry

Ferry Landing Park

Stockton

Mechanic St.

S. Main St.

Information center

New St.

Mule barge ride

Waterloo St.

Riverwoods Dr.

New Hope

N

19. Walton Road

A series of narrow bridges once spanned the Neshaminy Creek in central Bucks County, but over the years all but a few have washed out or been torn down, turning the roads leading to them into isolated dead-ends.

Walton Road at the southern edge of Warwick Township is one of these. It leads from Rushland Road to a small peninsula formed by a horseshoe bend in the creek. Cut off from the other side, this is a peaceful and secluded valley with a nice view of the creek. Conveniently, the ramp to the former bridge provides a place to park while you enjoy the scenery. (Be sure you aren't blocking the road or a nearby driveway before you leave your car.)

To reach this area, turn onto Walton from Rushland Road and proceed downhill past Wilkerson Road. Walton makes a sharp bend to the right, then ends at what looks like an intersection, though two of the arms are driveways and one is the bridge ramp.

The bottom of Walton is unpaved and runs quite close to the creek. After the first quarter of a mile from the end it is paved, but it remains relatively level for almost a mile until you come to the sharp bend, where it turns uphill. Walk as far as you like before turning back. If you get as far as Wilkerson, you'll find that it is also quite pretty and it doesn't carry much traffic, though it is somewhat hilly.

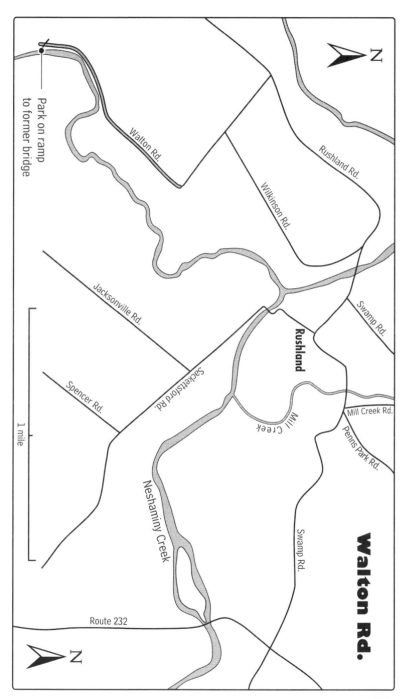

Park on ramp
to former bridge

Walton Rd.

Rushland Rd.

Wilkinson Rd.

Jacksonville Rd.

Spencer Rd.

Sacketsford Rd.

Rushland

Swamp Rd.

1 mile

Mill Creek

Mill Creek Rd.

Penns Park Rd.

Neshaminy Creek

Swamp Rd.

Walton Rd.

Route 232

N

N

20. Bowman's Hill

The Bowman's Hill Wildflower Preserve has some of the nicest wooded trails anywhere in Bucks County. Mostly gravel-covered and well maintained, they meander over hillsides and along a creek past nearly a thousand species of plants native to Pennsylvania.

The tall black fence around the eighty-acre preserve makes the place look like a private estate, but the barrier is intended to let everything in but the deer, who have been only too happy to demonstrate their appreciation for the native plant specimens.

My last visit to Bowman's Hill was on a gray winter day when I seemed to be the only human on the grounds, and the only sound that broke the silence was the rustle of squirrels scurrying through dry leaves. Suddenly, a metallic banging noise rang through the woods like a bell. I went toward it and found a deer butting its head against the fence, frustrated to be on the outside looking in at such a good thing. Fortunately, if you are human, getting past the fence is no big challenge. You simply pull up to the gate in your car, push the button that activates the automatic opener, and drive on through.

Inside, you'll find twenty-six trails traversing a variety of environments, including woods, meadows, and a bog. Pidcock Creek winds its way through the preserve, and a few of the trails follow its banks. Many of the trails are fairly level, while others go up and down following the contours of the hills beside the creek. The Woods Edge Trail is hard-paved and handicapped-accessible. The preserve is

BOWMAN'S HILL WILDFLOWER PRESERVE

River Rd. (Rte. 32)
near New Hope

Schedule: Visitor Center open 9 A.M. to 5 P.M. daily except Thanksgiving, Christmas, and New Year's Day

Terrain: Mostly hilly, with some level areas near the Visitor Center and along Pidcock Creek

Surface: Mostly gravel; Woods Edge Walk is paved and handicapped accessible

Info: 215.862.2924

rarely crowded, and its trails make for very pleasant walking, especially when things are in bloom.

You can pick up a trail map and some other free literature at the Visitor Center, where the Twinleaf Shop also offers T-shirts and books on nature and gardening. A native plant nursery produces seeds and live plants for the preserve, and these are also available for sale to the public.

Bowman's Hill Wildflower Preserve is located on Route 32 about two and a half miles south of New Hope. It is operated by a nonprofit association on state land that is officially part of the Washington Crossing Historic Park, although the main part of the park is located about four miles farther south (see page 64).

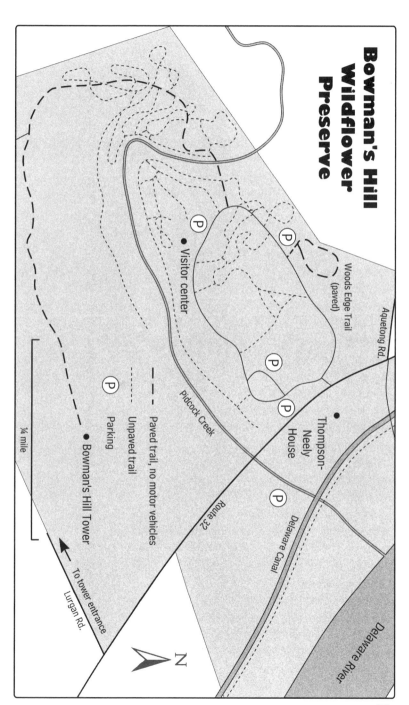

Bowman's Hill Wildflower Preserve

- Woods Edge Trail (paved)
- Aquetong Rd.
- Visitor center
- Thompson-Neely House
- Pidcock Creek
- Route 32
- Delaware Canal
- Delaware River
- Bowman's Hill Tower
- To tower entrance
- Lurgan Rd.
- ¼ mile
- N

Legend:
- – – – Paved trail, no motor vehicles
- ········ Unpaved trail
- (P) Parking

63

21. Washington Crossing

Every good student of American history knows the story about George Washington leading his men across the icy Delaware River on December 25, 1776, and defeating the holiday-weary Hessians in Trenton the next morning, changing the course of the Revolutionary War.

Washington Crossing Historic Park was created to promote the historic significance of the event through a documentary film, exhibits including a reproduction of Emanuel Leutze's famous painting of the crossing, and an annual reenactment on Christmas Day. The preserved town of Taylorsville includes several early nineteenth-century homes and businesses, as well as McConkey's Ferry Inn, where tradition says Washington dined before his boat ride. (See page 60 for information on the Thompson's Mill section of Washington Crossing Historic Park, located on Route 32 about three miles north.)

These days, of course, crossing the Delaware is no big deal. You'll find a bridge to New Jersey here, with another park on the other side where you can retrace some of Washington's route or create a walk of your own that combines both history and nature.

New Jersey's Washington Crossing State Park has another small collection of historic buildings and a Visitor Center, located about a mile from the Memorial Building and Visitor Center in Pennsylvania, with more interpretive displays. The larger park on the New Jersey side of the river also has recreational facilities including thirteen miles of hiking trails, a nature center, equestrian and mountain-bik-

WASHINGTON CROSSING HISTORIC PARK

Route 32
Washington Crossing, PA

Schedule: Buildings open Tuesday through Saturday 9 A.M. to 5 P.M.; Sunday noon to 5 P.M.; closed Monday and some holidays

Terrain: Level

Surface: Paved

Info: 215.493.4076

WASHINGTON CROSSING STATE PARK

Routes 29 & 546
Washington Crossing, NJ

Schedule: Nature center building open Wednesday through Saturday 9 A.M. to 4:30 P.M. , Sunday noon to 4:30 P.M. ; Visitor Center building open Wednesday through Sunday 9 A.M. to 4:30 P.M.

Terrain: Level to hilly

Surface: Paved paths, gravel trail, woodland trails

Info: 609.737.0623

ing trails, and camping areas. Continental Lane, now a footpath located between the two main paved park roads, was the route used by Washington's men as they marched on after the crossing.

Large park maps are posted at various locations in the New Jersey park. A printed version with detailed information on the trail system is available from racks attached to the signs.

Pennsylvania's Delaware Canal and New Jersey's Delaware and Raritan Canal run through the parks, and the canal paths offer further possibilities for extended walking. (See page 2.)

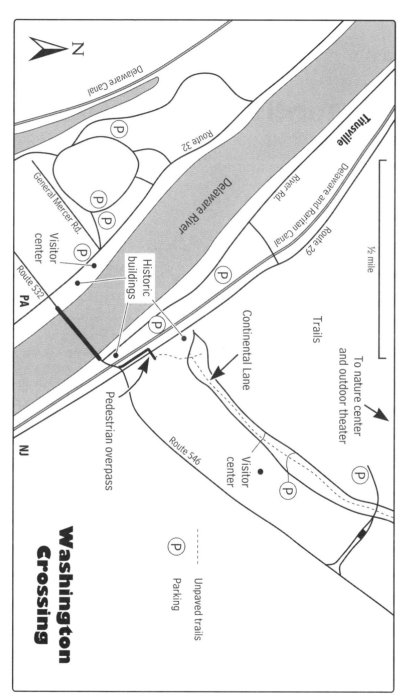

N

Delaware Canal

Route 32

General Mercer Rd.

Delaware River

Route 532

PA

NJ

Visitor center

Historic buildings

Trusville

Delaware and Raritan Canal

River Rd.

Route 29

Trails

½ mile

To nature center and outdoor theater

Continental Lane

Pedestrian overpass

Visitor center

Route 546

Washington Crossing

----- Unpaved trails

(P) Parking

67

22. Yardley

Yardley isn't as big as the other towns described in this book, and it doesn't have much in the way of formal attractions. It is, however, an extremely pretty little town that is perfectly deserving of attention if you're looking for a town walk.

The scenic center of town is Lake Afton, as graceful a pond as you'll see anywhere. It was built to serve the gristmill across Main Street and now serves for ice-skating in the winter and duck-feeding at other times. The Yardleyville Library, now the home of the Yardley Historical Association (215.493.9883), stands on an almost impossibly narrow strip of land beside the lake on West Afton Avenue, next to St. Andrew's Episcopal Church. (The historical association publishes a detailed Yardley walking tour, but it must be ordered from the organization by mail.)

If you walk from the old library building down Afton to the Delaware River, then back to the canal towpath, turn left at the canal to East College Avenue, right on College to South Main Street, right again on Main to Afton, and left to return to the library, you'll cover a distance of about 1.3 miles, passing many of the points of interest included in the tour.

Where Afton ends at the river, you'll find a ramp leading nowhere. Site of a bridge that once crossed to New Jersey, it is now maintained as a small park. Downriver from here, you can see the graceful arched stone bridge that carries the railroad across the river. Despite the lovely view, you won't want to do much walking here because there are no sidewalks or shoulders.

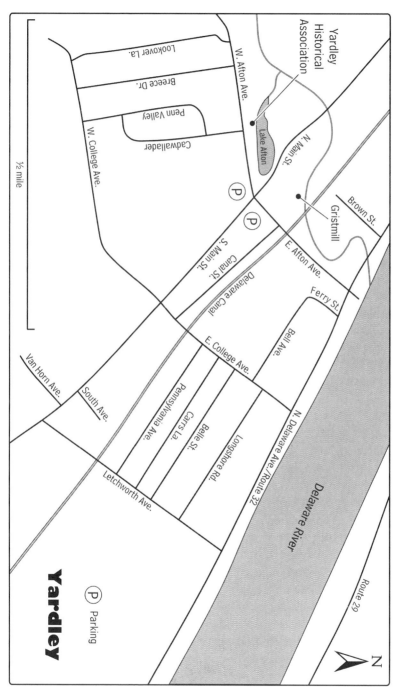

Yardley

Ⓟ Parking

N

½ mile

23. Tyler State Park

Tyler State Park is one of the most popular public recreation areas in Bucks County, and with good reason. It's a great place to walk, bike, ride a horse, paddle a canoe, picnic, ice skate, cross-country ski, or admire the view of Neshaminy Creek, which winds through the park.

Tyler officially lists about ten miles of paved bicycle trails, four miles of gravel hiking trails, and nine miles of equestrian trails. Hikers are allowed on all of them, and it's possible to put together a walk that's long or short, easy or more challenging, depending on your personal preferences.

Your first stop in the park should be at the park office near the main entrance, where you can pick up a copy of the latest trail map. The map in this book shows the park's major trails, but it is impossible at this scale to show the entire interwoven network of equestrian trails and smaller, unnamed walking trails. (The official map doesn't show the contours of the terrain, so keep in mind that most everything is uphill from the Neshaminy, especially on the west side.)

Looking for an easy walk? Park near the boathouse (which offers seasonal canoe rentals) and walk out and back along the creek on the Tyler Drive Trail. That will take you a total of about a mile and a quarter on a fairly level paved surface. Where the Tyler Drive Trail turns uphill and becomes the Quarry Trail, you can continue another third of a mile along the creek on an unpaved trail that looks like a wide, grassy lane. It leads to a good view of the dam across the Neshaminy.

To see this area from the other side of the creek, park at the fisherman's lot off Route 332 and follow what looks like an unpaved road between the trees at the end of the lawn next to the parking lot. It will bring you out to a good view of the dam from downstream; from here an unmapped trail goes north along the edge of the creek.

If you're in the mood for something more challenging, try a walk around the park. Leave your car near the boathouse, cross the causeway to the west side of the creek, and turn right. Following the Mill Dairy, White Pine, Dairy Hill, No. 1 Lane, and Stable Mill trails, you'll cover about six miles and see most of what Tyler has to offer: woods, cornfields, views of the Neshaminy from above and at water level, and a number of old stone farm buildings.

The Covered Bridge Trail leads past the hostel at the Solly House to the Schofield Ford Covered Bridge, which was destroyed by fire in 1991 but rebuilt by volunteers in 1997.

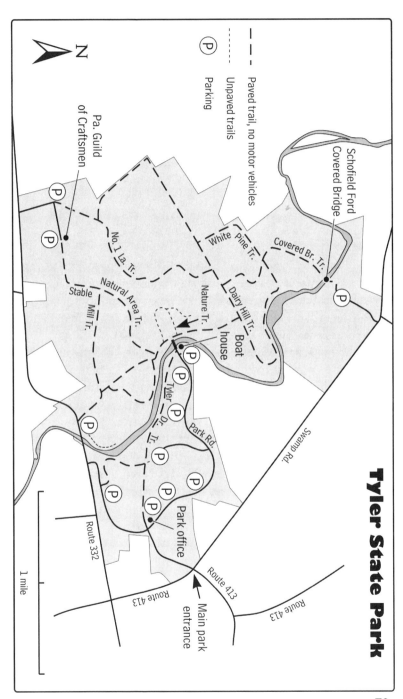

Tyler State Park

Legend:
- – – – Paved trail, no motor vehicles
- .... Unpaved trails
- (P) Parking

Pa. Guild of Craftsmen

Schofield Ford Covered Bridge

White Pine Tr.
Covered Br. Tr.
No. 1 La. Tr.
Natural Area Tr.
Stable
Mill Tr.
Dairy Hill Tr.
Nature Tr.
Boat house
Tyler Dr. Tr.
Park Rd.
Park office
Swamp Rd.
Route 332
Route 413
Route 413
Main park entrance

N

1 mile

24. Newtown

Peel away the layers from the onion that is Newtown and you'll pass from some of the most intense development now happening anywhere in Bucks County to a core that was laid out in 1684 by William Penn's surveyor, Thomas Holme (who also mapped out Penn's plans for a little town nearby called Philadelphia).

Newtown was the county seat of Bucks from 1725 through 1813, a fact that is relevant to the history of many of its oldest buildings. The Court Inn Museum (215.968.4004), located at the intersection of Court Street and Center Avenue and now the headquarters of the Newtown Historic Association, was a tavern and a popular hangout when the courthouse was across the street. You can pick up a copy of a detailed walking tour of Newtown there or at the Newtown Borough Council Chambers (215.968.2109) on North State Street.

The suggested walk outlined on this map covers a distance of about a mile and a half, starting at one of the municipal parking lots on Centre Street and making a loop through town and back again. It passes Newtown Commons, a small grassy park that was part of the area designated as public pasture on Holmes' original plan. Edward Hicks, the primitive painter who is best known for his Peaceable Kingdom paintings, lived on Penn Street and is buried in the Friends Burial Ground by the Friends Meetinghouse on Court Street.

A downtown area of shops and restaurants stretches along State Street between Green and Penn Streets.

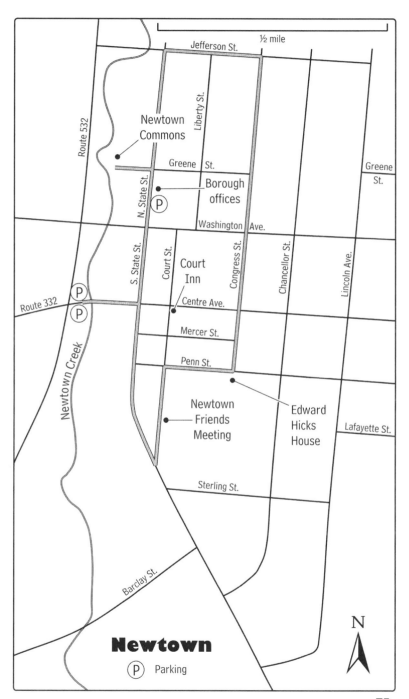

½ mile

Jefferson St.

Liberty St.

Route 532

Newtown
Commons

Greene St.

Greene
St.

N. State St.

Borough
offices

Washington Ave.

S. State St.

Court St.

Congress St.

Chancellor St.

Lincoln Ave.

Court
Inn

Centre Ave.

Route 332

Mercer St.

Penn St.

Newtown Creek

Edward
Hicks
House

Newtown
Friends
Meeting

Lafayette St.

Sterling St.

Barclay St.

N

Newtown

Ⓟ Parking

25. Core Creek

Core Creek Park is the headquarters of the Bucks County park system, and though it isn't as large as Peace Valley Park, the two have much in common. Like Peace Valley, Core Creek has a lake as its central feature, with a paved bike/hike path following its shoreline.

At Core Creek Park the lake is Lake Luxembourg, which extends from a dam not far from Route 413 to a final, slender finger fed by the stream called Core Creek on the east side of Woodbourne Road. The rest of the park is arranged to take advantage of it. There are fishing piers, a boat-launch ramp, and boat rentals, as well as picnic pavilions and strategically placed benches that capitalize on the beauty of the lake in a more passive way. Although St. Mary's Hospital and some nearby development houses are visible from parts of the park, woods, grassy fields, and the lake itself are all you see from most vantage points.

The paved bike/hike path is about a mile long. It begins at the end of the parking lot nearest the Tollgate Road entrance to the park. From there it wraps around a small hill down to the lake, winding in and out of the tree line and passing picnic pavilions, children's play areas, several baseball fields, and the boat ramp before ending at the park road, just before the dam. The path is about a mile long, but many people continue on the park road, going half a mile farther to the park headquarters near the Bridgetown Pike entrance. The restored nineteenth-century farmhouse also serves as the headquar-

CORE CREEK PARK

Between Tollgate Rd. and Bridgetown Pike
near Langhorne

Terrain: Gently rolling

Surface: Paved path; hiking allowed on unpaved equestrian
trails

ters for the entire Bucks County parks system, the second largest in the state of Pennsylvania.

On the other side of the lake there are tennis courts and more sports fields near a parking lot at Woodbourne Road. Most of this area is undeveloped, however, with the exception of some equestrian trails, which are sometimes used by hikers although they can be a little hard to follow.

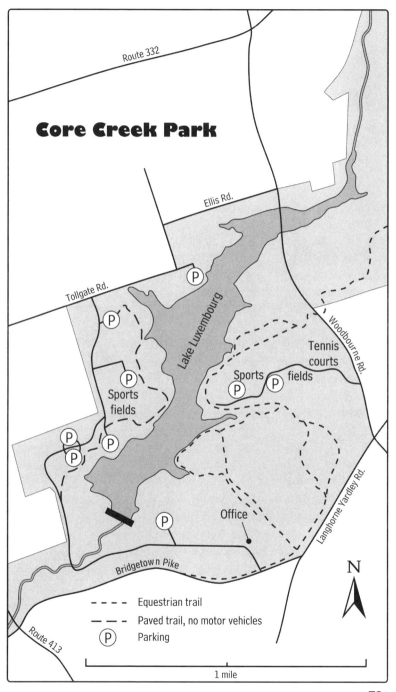

Core Creek Park

Route 332

Ellis Rd.

Tollgate Rd.

Lake Luxembourg

Woodbourne Rd.

(P)

(P)

(P)

(P) Sports fields

Tennis courts

Sports (P) fields

(P)

(P)

(P)

Langhorne Yardley Rd.

(P)

Office

Bridgetown Pike

Route 413

N

- - - - Equestrian trail
- - - Paved trail, no motor vehicles
(P) Parking

1 mile

26. Churchville Nature Center

Sitting on a bench at the edge of the trail by the Churchville Reservoir, watching honking geese take off and land without a house or road or any other evidence of civilization in sight, it would be possible to imagine yourself in some large and remote preserve instead of a small county park.

The Churchville Nature Center isn't a big place, yet it manages to foster a feeling of escape from the rest of busy lower Bucks County. It's true that you can see houses from some of the trails, but this is a peaceful place where the nearness of civilization doesn't really seem to matter.

There are only six trails here and they are mostly quite level, although they do go slightly uphill as you turn away from the reservoir and approach Elm Avenue. An overlook from the Deer Run Path provides a view of the reservoir. The Spring House Trail and the Leaf Down Trail also have views of the water.

You can pick up a copy of the detailed trail map at the nature center, which has interpretive exhibits and a gift shop. The first trail leaving the building is designed for handicapped access, and it is the only paved trail. Signs warn walkers not to leave the trails, which pass through a variety of environments including woods, a marsh, and a small pond. Benches are strategically placed around the trails.

As at the other nature centers in Bucks County parks, a variety of lectures and nature walks are offered here, including hands-on programs at the Lenape Village designed to show what life was like

CHURCHVILLE NATURE CENTER

501 Churchville La.
Churchville

Hours: Nature center building open Tuesday through Sunday 10 A.M. to 5 P.M.

Terrain: Level to gently uphill

Surface: Paved path, woodland trails

Info: 215.357.4005

among the Lenape Indians in the 1500s, just before Europeans began to arrive in the area.

Grandfather beech is a landmark worth looking for, a very large tree with many names carved on one side. Somewhat surprisingly, as well as unfortunately, the other side is quite hollow.

To get to the Churchville Nature Center from Route 532, turn north on Holland Road and make the next left onto Churchville Lane. The nature center is on the right about a quarter of a mile from the intersection of Churchville and Holland.

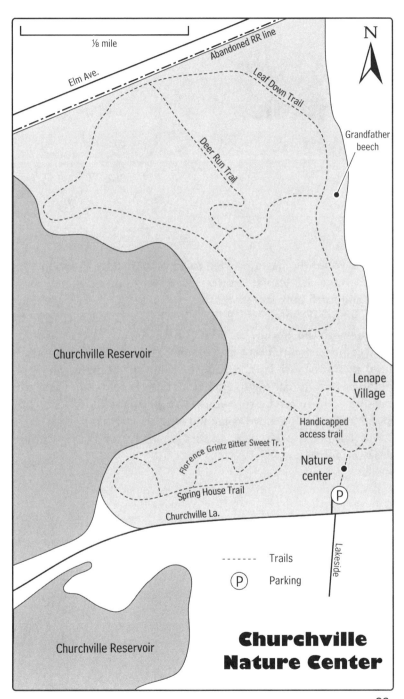

The malls

As anyone who has ever tried to accomplish a lot of shopping in a trip to the mall can attest, you can cover a lot distance walking back and forth between stores.

Your typical shopping mall might not have the scenic charm of a trail through the woods, but a lot of people who walk for exercise have come to realize that a mall has many advantages. The surface is level and never gets icy, and you won't find any potholes. The temperature remains constant whether it's bitterly cold or hot as blazes outside, and you can be sure you won't get rained on. You won't be alone, either. Both Oxford Valley and Neshaminy Malls open at 7 A.M. for walkers, and both have support programs for those who are really into mall walking.

27. Neshaminy Mall

Route 1 and Bristol Rd.
Bensalem

Hours: Monday through Thursday 10 A.M. to 9:30 P.M.; Friday and Saturday 10 A.M. to 10 P.M.; Sunday 11 A.M. to 7 P.M.; food court entrance opens at 7 A.M.

Program: Sign up for the walking program at the mall's customer service booth, where they'll keep track of the miles you've covered. One and half times around the outside edge of the hallways equals one mile.

Info: 215.357.6100

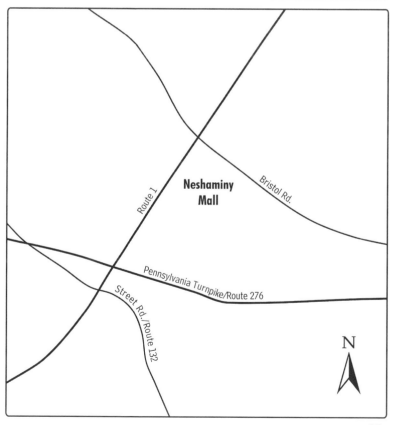

28. Oxford Valley Mall

2300 E. Lincoln Hwy.
Langhorne

Hours: Monday through Saturday 10 A.M. to 9 P.M.; Sunday 11 A.M. to 7 P.M.; food court entrance opens at 7 A.M.

Program: Oxford Valley Mall and Capital Health System sponsor a Mall Walkers Club, with regular meetings and educational lectures. A full loop of the mall's upper level equals half a mile. Details available from the mall's customer service booth.

Info: 215.752.0221

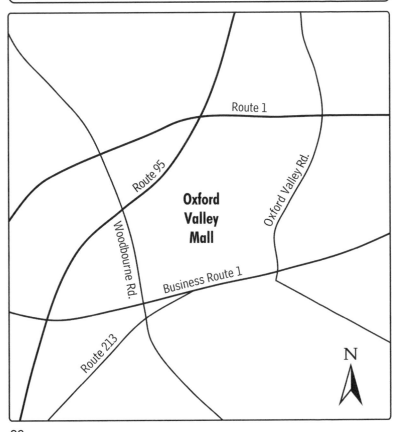

29. Five Mile Woods

When I was little, we lived in a housing development that backed up to a place we called "the woods." The land sloped down to a small creek, and from there you could look around in all directions and see trees. It seemed (to me at least) to go on forever.

We spent countless hours playing back there, constructing a series of ever-larger (but never ultimately successful) earthen dams across the creek. One day we left our shovels behind and went on a hiking expedition to look for the end of the woods, but we never did find it.

Five Mile Woods reminds me a lot of "the woods" of my childhood, though it's certainly bigger. This 285-acre nature preserve really deserves to be called a woods. Like my childhood refuge, however, it is right across the street from several developments, and I passed several families out walking the trails together the last time I was there. Even though you never completely escape traffic noise no matter how deeply you go into Five Miles Woods, it feels far, far away from those development houses and from busy Route 1, which runs quite near the southern border of the preserve.

A network of trails winds around the creeks here. A detailed trail map is posted on a board at the nature center, near the parking lot, and paper copies are available. The terrain is mostly level to very gently up and down, and the trails are well marked and well maintained. A canopy of trees keeps things relatively cool. Sturdy boardwalks and bridges have been constructed where necessary so you

FIVE MILE WOODS

1305 Big Oak Road
Lower Makefield

Terrain: Level to gently sloping

Surface: Woodland trails

Info: 215.493.3646

won't get your feet wet. The facilities also include an outdoor nature education area and a nature center building, although the building is not routinely left open.

Five Mile Woods is located near Route 95 and Route 1, but it can be a little tricky to find if you are not familiar with the area. The easiest way to get there is to head north on Oxford Valley Road from Oxford Valley Mall. Pass Route 1 and make the next right turn onto Big Oak Road. The entrance to the woods is on the right about a mile from the intersection of Big Oak Road and Oxford Valley Road.

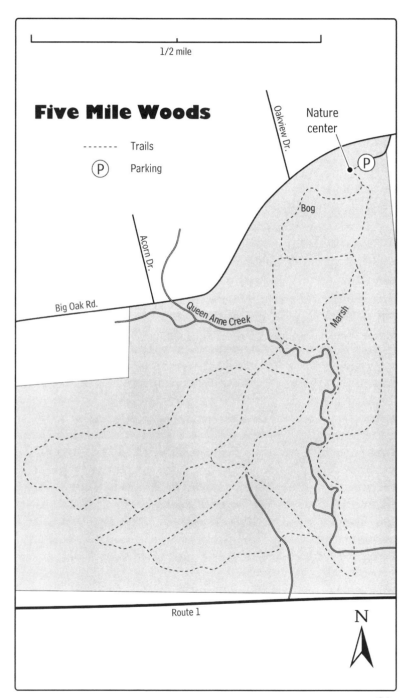

Five Mile Woods

- - - - - - Trails

(P) Parking

1/2 mile

Oakview Dr.

Nature center

Bog

Acorn Dr.

Big Oak Rd.

Queen Anne Creek

Marsh

Route 1

N

30. Neshaminy State Park

Two of the best things about the River Walk Trail at Neshaminy State Park are the educational trail guide available at the park office and the incredible view of the Philadelphia skyline from Logan Point.

The park is located on the Delaware River at the mouth of Neshaminy Creek. (To get there, take the Street Road exit from Route 95 and follow signs.) Its facilities include a swimming pool, picnic areas, and a 250-slip marina across the creek from the main section of the park. A tree-lined, paved path called Logan Walk is about a mile and a half long and connects the largest parking lots, the Playmaster Theater, and several picnic areas.

For walkers, the River Walk Trail is the main attraction. The trail has two loops: The outer section is about a mile and a half long and follows closer to the shoreline, while the inner trail is shorter and swings through the interior of the park. You can pick up an illustrated brochure describing the trail at the park office, where an overall map of the park is also available. The trail brochure seems to have been created with children in mind, but it is interesting and informative for adults, as well.

Logan Point, located near the end of the paved road that passes the park office, is not the official trailhead but it's a good place to start your walk. It has a panoramic view of the river and the houses perched in a row along the riverbank on the New Jersey side. The view down river includes the office towers of Center City Philadelphia, which appear to rise rather dramatically from the water itself.

NESHAMINY STATE PARK

3401 State Road
Bensalem

Terrain: Level to gently sloping

Surface: Paved paths, gravel, dirt, and soft sand

Info: 215.639.4538

A row of park benches is strategically arranged for those who wish to sit and admire the view.

As strange as it might seem, the Delaware River is tidal here, creating a marsh that is flooded twice a day and provides homes for a variety of plants and animals. When the tide is out, you can walk along a narrow sandy beach looking for smooth rocks and clam and mussel shells. (Just don't be tempted to take a quick dip; rows of red signs emphatically warn that swimming here is forbidden.)

When the asphalt path bends away from the river past Logan Point, the River Walk trail continues straight ahead along the shoreline. It is only a faint trace at first and it can be a little hard to find, though it becomes more obvious as you go forward into the woods.

For those who care to explore, the River Walk brochure has information about other plants and animals that make this environment their home. On a recent walk, I saw deer, ducks, and squirrels without trying very hard.

Unfortunately, I also saw a good collection of trash left behind at the river's edge when the tide receded. Although this is a pleasant walk, it suffers from the feeling that you never really get very far from civilization. You can hear the hum of highway noise in the most isolated parts of the park, and the marina and swimming pool draw many human visitors in the summer.

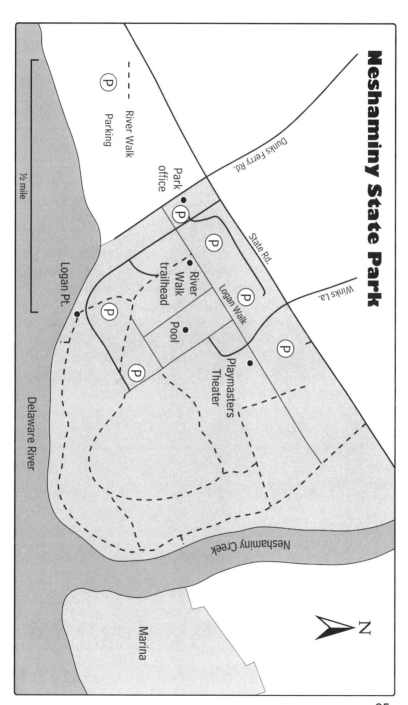

Neshaminy State Park

Dunks Ferry Rd.

State Rd.

Winks La.

Logan Walk

Park office

River Walk trailhead

Pool

Playmasters Theater

Logan Pt.

Delaware River

Neshaminy Creek

Marina

N

- - - - - River Walk

P Parking

½ mile

3 1. Silver Lake Park

Sometimes the beauty of a place becomes most apparent when it is compared to its surroundings.

Silver Lake's location is less than promising, given its proximity to Route 13, the Pennsylvania Turnpike, and Bath Road in a rather densely developed area of lower Bucks County. The honking of geese on the south end of the lake doesn't quite drown out the traffic noise from the busy roads nearby, but still the place manages to have the peaceful feeling of a world apart.

The county facilities at Silver Lake are divided into several sections. The southern part, at the intersection of Route 13 and Bath Road, includes a public recreation area with parking, a small playground, barbecue grills, and picnic tables. A paved path runs about a mile around the bottom of the lake. At times this part of the park can become quite congested, but when it is not too busy the trail makes a lovely walk with a pleasing view of the lake. The last time I was there, on a soft fall afternoon, I shared the shore area with a birdwatcher equipped with a fancy pair of binoculars, and we watched a hawk slowly and gracefully circle above.

North of the recreation area is the Silver Lake Nature Center, operated cooperatively by the county and the Friends of Silver Lake Nature Center. Its 235 acres include deep woods, fields, and broad wetlands, with a four-mile network of well maintained trails and boardwalks with raised platforms to provide better viewing in some

SILVER LAKE NATURE CENTER

1306 Bath Road
Bristol

Hours: Nature center building open Tuesday through Saturday 10 A.M. to 5 P.M., Sunday noon to 5 P.M.

Terrain: Level

Surface: Paved paths, woodland trails

Info 215.785.1177

areas. The paths run along the lake and into wetlands that are popular with birdwatchers.

A lakeside trail begins at the northern end of the recreation area, but the nature center has its own parking and access to trails farther north on Bath Road. A trail across Bath Road from the nature center leads into Delhaas Woods, said to be the best remaining example of the Atlantic Coastal Plain forest left in the state of Pennsylvania.

The nature center building has a gift shop that sells nature books, T-shirts, and activity sets, among other things. The building is the base for guided walks and talks, and it has exhibits explaining the Atlantic Coastal Plain environment and the plants and animals that can be found around Silver Lake. You can pick up a copy of a detailed trail map there, too.

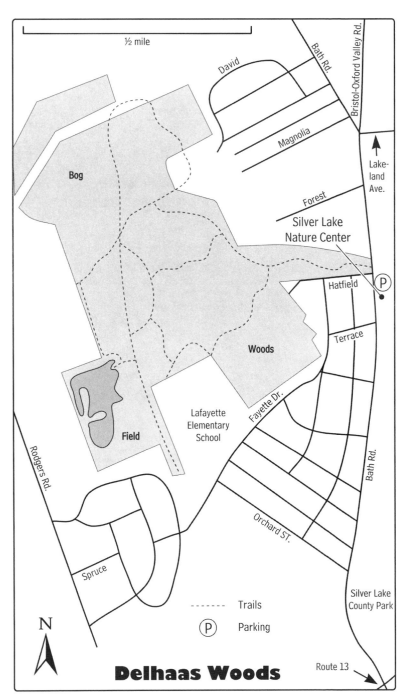

½ mile

David

Bath Rd.

Bristol-Oxford Valley Rd.

Magnolia

Lake-
land
Ave.

Forest

Bog

Silver Lake
Nature Center

Hatfield

Terrace

Woods

Fayette Dr.

Rodgers Rd.

Field

Lafayette
Elementary
School

Bath Rd.

Orchard ST.

Spruce

Silver Lake
County Park

Trails

P Parking

N

Delhaas Woods

Route 13

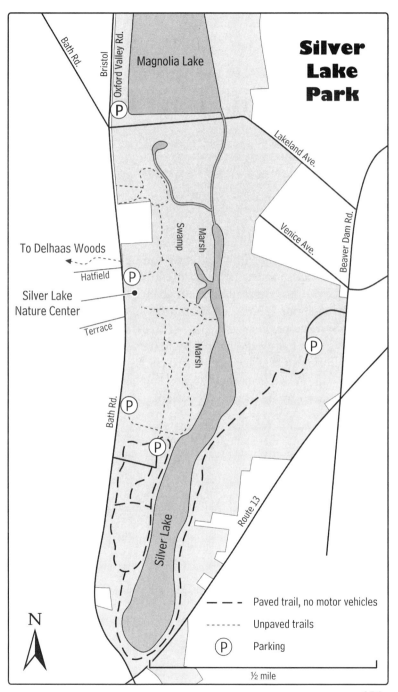

Silver Lake Park

Magnolia Lake

Bath Rd.

Bristol

Oxford Valley Rd.

Lakeland Ave.

Venice Ave.

Beaver Dam Rd.

Swamp

Marsh

Marsh

To Delhaas Woods

Hatfield

Silver Lake
Nature Center

Terrace

Bath Rd.

Route 13

Silver Lake

N

- - - Paved trail, no motor vehicles

.... Unpaved trails

P Parking

½ mile

32. Bristol Spurline

The Bristol Spurline Trail is a good example of using a trail to connect neighborhoods and bring an entire town closer together.

The trail follows the course of an abandoned rail line in Bristol Borough. It is mostly surfaced in asphalt and extends for a total of about two miles, passing parks, playing fields, and several schools.

The western half of the path is broken up by a number of cross streets, although it is still very useful to children, among others, who use it to walk to and from their homes. If you are walking for recreation instead of trying to get somewhere in particular, you may enjoy sticking to the eastern section.

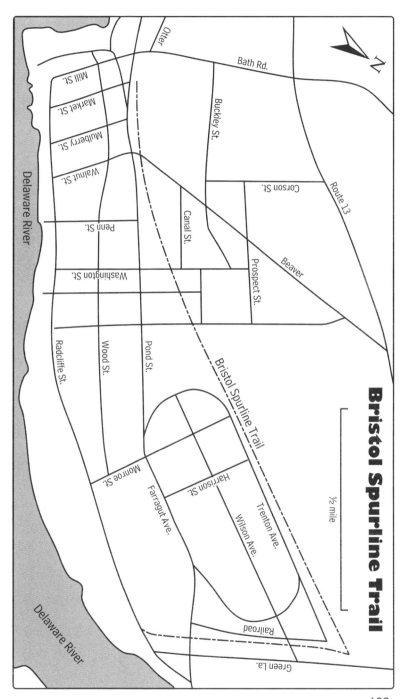

Bristol Spurline Trail

½ mile

Town & road walks

Paved paths

Unpaved trails

My walks

Date: _____
Place: _____
Comments: _____
_____
_____
_____

Date: _____
Place: _____
Comments: _____
_____
_____
_____

Date: _____
Place: _____
Comments: _____
_____
_____
_____

Date: _____
Place: _____
Comments: _____
_____
_____
_____

Date: _____
Place: _____
Comments: _____
_____
_____

My walks

Date:
Place:
Comments:

Date:
Place:
Comments:

Date:
Place:
Comments:

Date:
Place:
Comments:

Date:
Place:
Comments:

My walks

Date:
Place:
Comments:

Date:
Place:
Comments:

Date:
Place:
Comments:

Date:
Place:
Comments:

Date:
Place:
Comments:

My walks

Date:
Place:
Comments:

Date:
Place:
Comments:

Date:
Place:
Comments:

Date:
Place:
Comments:

Date:
Place:
Comments:

My walks

Date: _____
Place: _____
Comments: _____
_____
_____
_____

Date: _____
Place: _____
Comments: _____
_____
_____
_____

Date: _____
Place: _____
Comments: _____
_____
_____
_____

Date: _____
Place: _____
Comments: _____
_____
_____
_____

Date: _____
Place: _____
Comments: _____
_____
_____

My walks

Date:
Place:
Comments:

Date:
Place:
Comments:

Date:
Place:
Comments:

Date:
Place:
Comments:

Date:
Place:
Comments:

My walks

Date:
Place:
Comments:

Date:
Place:
Comments:

Date:
Place:
Comments:

Date:
Place:
Comments:

Date:
Place:
Comments:

My walks

Date:
Place:
Comments:

Date:
Place:
Comments:

Date:
Place:
Comments:

Date:
Place:
Comments:

Date:
Place:
Comments:

My walks

Date: _____
Place: _____
Comments: _____
_____
_____
_____

Date: _____
Place: _____
Comments: _____
_____
_____
_____

Date: _____
Place: _____
Comments: _____
_____
_____
_____

Date: _____
Place: _____
Comments: _____
_____
_____
_____

Date: _____
Place: _____
Comments: _____
_____
_____

Buy a book

Use this form to order books from Freewheeling Press, or look for more information about ordering online at www.freewheelingpress.com.

Name:			
Address:			
Telephone:			

No.	Title	Price	Total
	Walking Bucks County, Pa. A guide to walks on country roads, paved paths, and woodland trails in this scenic area, with maps.	$12.95	
	Mountain Biking in New Jersey 37 off-road rides in the Garden State, each accompanied by descriptive text and a detailed map with everything you need to know to enjoy each ride.	$13.95	
	Freewheeling Press Bike Journal Personal bike touring journal opens flat for easy writing, with space to record directions, distance, difficulty, and other details of your rides.	$12.95	
	Back Roads Bicycling in Bucks County, Pa. Features rides ranging in length from 7.9 to 47.1 miles; includes information on bike paths and local cycling clubs in this popular area.	$12.95	
	The Back Roads Bike Book Maps and directions for a dozen short scenic rides in and around Lambertville, N.J., and New Hope, Pa., with info on things to see and do, places to stay.	$12.95	

Send to: **Freewheeling Press** **PO Box 540** **Lahaska PA 18931**	Shipping ($2 per book)	
	Subtotal	
	Pa. residents add 6% tax	
	Grand total	
	Make check payable to Freewheeling Press	